Smartly Track your Goals to Superior Achievements with Ease

Your smart "GPS" to keep you on track to your targeted goals

Smartly Track your Goals to Superior Achievements with Ease

Your smart "GPS" to keep you on track to your targeted goals

Frank S. Adamo

Printed by CreateSpace, An Amazon.com Company
CreateSpace, Charleston SC

Copyright © 2013 by Frank S. Adamo

All rights reserved. This book or any portion thereof may
not be reproduced or used in any manner whatsoever,
including photocopying, recording, or other electronic
or mechanical methods, without the express
written permission of the author, except
as provided by USA copyright law.

Quantity Sales

Special discounts are available on
quantity purchases by corporations,
businesses, associations, and others.
For details, contact the author at
frank@fsadamo.com or 1-714-408-9287.

Printed in the United States of America

ISBN 978-1494774097

Quality Communications & Training
Cypress, CA 90630
www.QualityCommunications.org

Setting your Goals

Set a Vision for the Year

_____
_____
_____
_____
_____
_____

Set a Yearly Goal

_____
_____
_____
_____
_____
_____

Specific Tasks you want to complete within a year

Personal	Career
_____	_____
_____	_____
_____	_____
_____	_____
_____	_____
_____	_____

Frank S. Adamo   frank@fsadamo.com   1-714-408-9287

Week 1

"You weren't an accident, you weren't mass produced. You aren't an assembly-line product. You were deliberately planned, specifically gifted, and lovingly positioned on the Earth by the Master Craftsman."

— Max Lucado

Michelangelo did not create David. He found a slab of marble that God created and he translated that slab into a beautiful sculpture of David. You may have the same message or goal as others, yet you will sculpture your slab of marble differently for others. Set your goals to fit you specific interpretation of your needs.

Your goal this week _____

_____

_____

_____

Did you accomplish your goal? Yes ☐ No ☐

If yes, how do you feel? _____

_____

_____

If not, explain why and what else you can do to achieve your goal _____

_____

_____

Other comments _____

_____

_____

Daily Steps

Day 1 _____
_____
_____
_____

Day 2 _____
_____
_____
_____

Day 3 _____
_____
_____
_____

Day 4 _____
_____
_____
_____

Day 5 _____
_____
_____
_____

Day 6 _____
_____
_____
_____

Day 7 _____
_____
_____
_____

Frank S. Adamo frank@fsadamo.com 714-408-9287

Week 2

"Go within every day and find the inner strength so that the world will not blow your candle out."

— Katherine Dunham

Adversities of every kind affect all of us. Many minor obstacles and some major tragedies will occur. We need to face them and stand tall. We all have the power to keep our candle lit as we pass through these troubled times by discovering our inner strength

Your goal this week _____

_____

_____

_____

Did you accomplish your goal? Yes ☐ No ☐

If yes, how do you feel? _____

_____

_____

If not, explain why and what else you can do to achieve your goal _____

_____

_____

Other comments _____

_____

_____

_____

_____

_____

Daily Steps

Day 1 _____

_____

_____

_____

Day 2 _____

_____

_____

_____

Day 3 _____

_____

_____

_____

Day 4 _____

_____

_____

_____

Day 5 _____

_____

_____

_____

Day 6 _____

_____

_____

_____

Day 7 _____

_____

_____

_____

Frank S. Adamo   frank@fsadamo.com   714-408-9287

Week 3

"God, grant me the serenity to accept the things I cannot change, the courage to change the things I can, and the wisdom to know the difference"

— Reinhold Niebuhr

Regardless, if you are religious or not, the intent is the same. We can't change the past. We can't change the outcome of death or other tragedies. However, we can have the courage to struggle through and grow from our adversities.

Your goal this week _____

_____

_____

_____

Did you accomplish your goal? Yes ☐ No ☐

If yes, how do you feel? _____

_____

_____

If not, explain why and what else you can do to achieve your goal _____

_____

_____

Other comments _____

_____

_____

_____

_____

_____

Daily Steps

Day 1 _____
_____
_____
_____

Day 2 _____
_____
_____
_____

Day 3 _____
_____
_____
_____

Day 4 _____
_____
_____
_____

Day 5 _____
_____
_____
_____

Day 6 _____
_____
_____
_____

Day 7 _____
_____
_____
_____

Frank S. Adamo   frank@fsadamo.com   714-408-9287

Week 4

"You are what you think"

— Abraham Lincoln

The Law of Attraction states that your mind will attract what you think. What ever you think, you are. If you think you are poor, you are poor. Many winners of the Lotto will lose their millions of dollars if you think and act like you are wealthy, you will be healthy. If you think you are dumb, you will be dumb. If you think you are the smartest person on your block, you will be.

Your goal this week _____

_____

_____

Did you accomplish your goal? Yes ☐ No ☐

If yes, how do you feel? _____

_____

_____

If not, explain why and what else you can do to achieve your goal _____

_____

_____

Other comments _____

_____

_____

_____

_____

Daily Steps

Day 1 _____

_____

_____

_____

Day 2 _____

_____

_____

_____

Day 3 _____

_____

_____

_____

Day 4 _____

_____

_____

_____

Day 5 _____

_____

_____

_____

Day 6 _____

_____

_____

_____

Day 7 _____

_____

_____

Frank S. Adamo   frank@fsadamo.com   714-408-9287

Week 5

"You can not always control circumstances, but you can control your own thoughts."

— C Popplestown.

As per the Serenity Prayer, accept the things we cannot change, the courage to change the things we can, and the wisdom to know the difference. Too often, our thoughts are occupied on the things we can't change, a natural disaster, a sudden death in the family, the results of an election, etc. Concentrate on what we can learn from adversity and change what we can. We can definitely change our thoughts.

Your goal this week _____

_____

_____

_____

Did you accomplish your goal? Yes ☐ No ☐

If yes, how do you feel? _____

_____

_____

If not, explain why and what else you can do to achieve your goal _____

_____

_____

Other comments _____

_____

_____

_____

_____

Daily Steps

Day 1 _____

_____

_____

_____

Day 2 _____

_____

_____

_____

Day 3 _____

_____

_____

_____

Day 4 _____

_____

_____

_____

Day 5 _____

_____

_____

_____

Day 6 _____

_____

_____

_____

Day 7 _____

_____

_____

_____

Frank S. Adamo   frank@fsadamo.com   714-408-9287

Week 6

"If you think you can or you think you can't, you're right."
— Henry Ford

Whatever you think will happen. If you have lost your job and you are thinking it will be so difficult to find another, it will be more difficult. If you are thinking that this is a great time to be with my family while I find a better position, you will be right.

Your goal this week _____

_____

_____

_____

Did you accomplish your goal? Yes ☐ No ☐

If yes, how do you feel? _____

_____

_____

If not, explain why and what else you can do to achieve your goal _____

_____

_____

Other comments _____

_____

_____

_____

_____

_____

_____

Daily Steps
Day 1 _____
Day 2 _____
Day 3 _____
Day 4 _____
Day 5 _____
Day 6 _____
Day 7 _____

Frank S. Adamo   frank@fsadamo.com   714-408-9287

Week 7

"Nobody can make you feel inferior without your consent."
— Eleanor Roosevelt

Children can be terribly abusive in what they say to others. This can be carried on in adulthood. You simply need to understand that you are unique and a wonderful person. It's the other person who tries to make you feel inferior who has the problem—not you. You may have heard, "Sticks and stones may break my bones, but words will never hurt." What? Broken bones can heal over time, but words may never heal—unless you DON'T give them permission.

Your goal this week _____

_____

_____

Did you accomplish your goal? Yes ☐ No ☐

If yes, how do you feel? _____

_____

_____

If not, explain why and what else you can do to achieve your goal ____

_____

_____

Other comments _____

_____

_____

_____

_____

Frank S. Adamo   frank@fsadamo.com   714-408-9287

Daily Steps

Day 1 _____
_____
_____
_____

Day 2 _____
_____
_____
_____

Day 3 _____
_____
_____
_____

Day 4 _____
_____
_____
_____

Day 5 _____
_____
_____
_____

Day 6 _____
_____
_____
_____

Day 7 _____
_____
_____
_____

Week 8

"Before you begin a thing, remind yourself that difficulties and delays quite impossible to foresee are ahead... You can only see one thing clearly, and that is your goal. Form a mental vision of that and cling to it through thick and thin."

— -- Kathleen Norris

Focus on the present while maintaining the vision of what will be. Also, don't look backwards and consider, "what's the use." Some people believe that Thomas Edison failed 10,000 times before he invented the light bulb. Truthfully, he never failed. He would have failed only if, up to the 9,999th time, he gave up. Don't give up. Persevere.

Your goal this week_____

_____

_____

_____

Did you accomplish your goal? Yes ☐ No ☐

If yes, how do you feel? _____

_____

_____

If not, explain why and what else you can do to achieve your goal_____

_____

_____

Other comments_____

_____

_____

_____

Frank S. Adamo   frank@fsadamo.com   714-408-9287

Daily Steps

Day 1 _____
_____
_____
_____

Day 2 _____
_____
_____
_____

Day 3 _____
_____
_____
_____

Day 4 _____
_____
_____
_____

Day 5 _____
_____
_____
_____

Day 6 _____
_____
_____
_____

Day 7 _____
_____
_____
_____

Week 9

"This one step - choosing a goal and sticking to it - changes everything."

— Scott Reed

At one point or another in our lives, most of us will become content where we are and our ultimate dreams will fade away. Make a goal that will set you back on track to achieving your dreams, and stick with it until you achieve your dreams.

Your goal this week _____

_____

_____

_____

Did you accomplish your goal? Yes ☐ No ☐

If yes, how do you feel? _____

_____

_____

If not, explain why and what else you can do to achieve your goal _____

_____

_____

Other comments _____

_____

_____

_____

_____

_____

Daily Steps

Day 1 _____

_____

_____

_____

Day 2 _____

_____

_____

_____

Day 3 _____

_____

_____

_____

Day 4 _____

_____

_____

_____

Day 5 _____

_____

_____

_____

Day 6 _____

_____

_____

_____

Day 7 _____

_____

_____

_____

Frank S. Adamo frank@fsadamo.com 714-408-9287

Week 10

"Time is more value than money. You can get more money, but you cannot get more time."

— Jim Rohn

The purpose of setting goal(s) is to stay on track and not procrastinate. The purpose of this workbook is create a yearly goal and then to take weekly steps to achieving your goal.

Your goal this week _____

_____

_____

_____

Did you accomplish your goal? Yes ☐ No ☐

If yes, how do you feel? _____

_____

_____

If not, explain why and what else you can do to achieve your goal _____

_____

_____

Other comments _____

_____

_____

_____

_____

_____

Daily Steps

Day 1 _____

_____

_____

_____

Day 2 _____

_____

_____

_____

Day 3 _____

_____

_____

_____

Day 4 _____

_____

_____

_____

Day 5 _____

_____

_____

_____

Day 6 _____

_____

_____

_____

Day 7 _____

_____

_____

_____

Frank S. Adamo   frank@fsadamo.com   714-408-9287

Week 11

"We either make ourselves miserable or we make ourselves strong. The amount of work is the same."
— Carlos Castaneda

Focus on the positive, even if you have setbacks. Persevere through the setbacks and personal adversities. Learning from our mistakes and going forward is how we grow.

Your goal this week _____

_____

_____

_____

Did you accomplish your goal? Yes ☐ No ☐

If yes, how do you feel? _____

_____

_____

If not, explain why and what else you can do to achieve your goal ____

_____

_____

Other comments _____

_____

_____

_____

_____

_____

_____

Daily Steps
Day 1 _____
Day 2 _____
Day 3 _____
Day 4 _____
Day 5 _____
Day 6 _____
Day 7 _____

Frank S. Adamo   frank@fsadamo.com   714-408-9287

Week 12

"Until you make peace with who you are you will never be content with what you have."

— Doris Mortman

If you stay focus on your goals and you understand who you are, you will succeed. Too often, we grow up not really understanding who we are. Sure we have your family and friends, but do you really understand who you are? We ware the accumulation of our parents, grandparents, great grandparents, and on an on, back to our ancestry. Learn about you heritage and realize this is part of you. If you are adopted, you can determine your true heritage with a DNA test.

Your goal this week _____

_____

_____

_____

Did you accomplish your goal? Yes ☐ No ☐

If yes, how do you feel? _____

_____

_____

If not, explain why and what else you can do to achieve your goal _____

_____

_____

Other comments _____

_____

_____

_____

_____

Daily Steps

Day 1 _____

Day 2 _____

Day 3 _____

Day 4 _____

Day 5 _____

Day 6 _____

Day 7 _____

Frank S. Adamo	frank@fsadamo.com	714-408-9287

Week 13

"Rowing harder doesn't help if the boat is headed in the wrong direction."

— Kenichi Ohmae

Be sure you stay focus on your vision and your plan (goals) to get there. Stay in the present while visualizing the finish line.

Your goal this week _____

_____

_____

_____

Did you accomplish your goal? Yes ☐ No ☐

If yes, how do you feel? _____

_____

_____

If not, explain why and what else you can do to achieve your goal _____

_____

_____

Other comments _____

_____

_____

_____

_____

_____

_____

Daily Steps

Day 1 _____
_____
_____
_____

Day 2 _____
_____
_____
_____

Day 3 _____
_____
_____
_____

Day 4 _____
_____
_____
_____

Day 5 _____
_____
_____
_____

Day 6 _____
_____
_____
_____

Day 7 _____
_____
_____
_____

Frank S. Adamo   frank@fsadamo.com   714-408-9287

Week 14

"Being powerful is like being a lady. If you have to tell people you are, you aren't"

— Margaret Thatcher

True leaders do not need to brag. They also accept responsibility.

Your goal this week _____

_____

_____

_____

Did you accomplish your goal? Yes ☐ No ☐

If yes, how do you feel? _____

_____

_____

If not, explain why and what else you can do to achieve your goal _____

_____

_____

Other comments _____

_____

_____

_____

_____

_____

_____

_____

Daily Steps

Day 1 _____
_____
_____
_____

Day 2 _____
_____
_____
_____

Day 3 _____
_____
_____
_____

Day 4 _____
_____
_____
_____

Day 5 _____
_____
_____
_____

Day 6 _____
_____
_____
_____

Day 7 _____
_____
_____
_____

Frank S. Adamo   frank@fsadamo.com   714-408-9287

Week 15

"A goal without a plan is just a wish."

— Larry Elder

Make you wishes come true by planning a course of action. Stay on course and continue your plan no matter what obstacles you encounter.

Your goal this week _____

_____

_____

_____

Did you accomplish your goal? Yes ☐ No ☐

If yes, how do you feel? _____

_____

_____

If not, explain why and what else you can do to achieve your goal _____

_____

_____

Other comments _____

_____

_____

_____

_____

_____

_____

_____

Frank S. Adamo   frank@fsadamo.com

Daily Steps

Day 1 _____
_____
_____
_____

Day 2 _____
_____
_____
_____

Day 3 _____
_____
_____
_____

Day 4 _____
_____
_____
_____

Day 5 _____
_____
_____
_____

Day 6 _____
_____
_____
_____

Day 7 _____
_____
_____
_____

714-408-9287

Week 16

"Obstacles cannot crush me. Every obstacle yields to stern resolve."
— Leonardo da Vinci

Obstacles will crush you only if you they stop you from succeeding. You will always encounter obstacles; however, you can always climb over or go around the obstacles. Just stay resolved to get back on track to your destination.

Your goal this week _____

_____

_____

_____

Did you accomplish your goal? Yes ☐ No ☐

If yes, how do you feel? _____

_____

_____

If not, explain why and what else you can do to achieve your goal _____

_____

_____

Other comments _____

_____

_____

_____

_____

_____

Daily Steps
Day 1 _____
_____
_____
_____
Day 2 _____
_____
_____
_____
Day 3 _____
_____
_____
_____
Day 4 _____
_____
_____
_____
Day 5 _____
_____
_____
_____
Day 6 _____
_____
_____
_____
Day 7 _____
_____
_____
_____

Frank S. Adamo   frank@fsadamo.com   714-408-9287

Week 17

"There are a lot of people whose fires are there but need a little poking,"
— Ralph Wardo Emerson

Can you poke a friend? Do you need poking? A way to keep poking the fire beneath you and your friends is to start a small mastermind group.

Your goal this week _____

_____

_____

_____

Did you accomplish your goal? Yes ☐ No ☐

If yes, how do you feel? _____

_____

_____

If not, explain why and what else you can do to achieve your goal _____

_____

_____

Other comments _____

_____

_____

_____

_____

_____

_____

Frank S. Adamo   frank@fsadamo.com   714-408-9287

Daily Steps
Day 1 _____
Day 2 _____
Day 3 _____
Day 4 _____
Day 5 _____
Day 6 _____
Day 7 _____

Week 18

"View change as the one constant in your life. Welcome it. Expect it. Anticipate it."

— Denis Waitley

Yet, some change is not for the better. Expect it. Anticipate it. However, welcome it, only if it's for the betterment of you and mankind. If not, start a new change.

Your goal this week _____

_____

_____

_____

Did you accomplish your goal? Yes ☐ No ☐

If yes, how do you feel? _____

_____

_____

If not, explain why and what else you can do to achieve your goal _____

_____

_____

Other comments _____

_____

_____

_____

_____

_____

_____

Daily Steps
Day 1 _____
Day 2 _____
Day 3 _____
Day 4 _____
Day 5 _____
Day 6 _____
Day 7 _____

Frank S. Adamo		frank@fsadamo.com		714-408-9287

Week 19

"The only job where you start at the top, is digging a hole"
— Anonymous

Don't get caught digging a hole. Life is about reaching forward and upward, never backwards or downwards.

Your goal this week _____

_____

_____

_____

Did you accomplish your goal? Yes ☐ No ☐

If yes, how do you feel? _____

_____

_____

If not, explain why and what else you can do to achieve your goal _____

_____

_____

Other comments _____

_____

_____

_____

_____

_____

_____

Daily Steps
Day 1 _____
Day 2 _____
Day 3 _____
Day 4 _____
Day 5 _____
Day 6 _____
Day 7 _____

Frank S. Adamo   frank@fsadamo.com   714-408-9287

Week 20

"The simple act of paying positive attention to people has a great deal to do with productivity."
— Tom Peters

Always focus on your own positive attributes. Don't let others dictate what you will be or what you will accomplish.

Your goal this week _____

_____

_____

_____

Did you accomplish your goal? Yes ☐ No ☐

If yes, how do you feel? _____

_____

_____

If not, explain why and what else you can do to achieve your goal _____

_____

_____

Other comments _____

_____

_____

_____

_____

_____

_____

Daily Steps

Day 1 _____
_____
_____
_____

Day 2 _____
_____
_____
_____

Day 3 _____
_____
_____
_____

Day 4 _____
_____
_____
_____

Day 5 _____
_____
_____
_____

Day 6 _____
_____
_____
_____

Day 7 _____
_____
_____
_____

Frank S. Adamo   frank@fsadamo.com   714-408-9287

Week 21

"If you accept a limiting belief, then it will become a truth for you."

— Louise Hay

Don't limit your thoughts and dreams. Instead, make them limitless.

Your goal this week _____

_____

_____

_____

Did you accomplish your goal? Yes ☐ No ☐

If yes, how do you feel? _____

_____

_____

If not, explain why and what else you can do to achieve your goal _____

_____

_____

Other comments _____

_____

_____

_____

_____

_____

_____

Daily Steps
Day 1 _____
Day 2 _____
Day 3 _____
Day 4 _____
Day 5 _____
Day 6 _____
Day 7 _____

Frank S. Adamo   frank@fsadamo.com   714-408-9287

Week 22

"It is easy to sit up and take notice. What is difficult is getting up and taking action.

— Al Batt

Like Dionne Warwick's song, "Wishin' and hopin' and thinkin' and prayin' plannin' and dreamin' each night of his charms. That won't get you into his arms." You cannot pursue your dreams and aspirations if you don't take action.

Your goal this week _____

_____

_____

_____

Did you accomplish your goal? Yes ☐ No ☐

If yes, how do you feel? _____

_____

_____

If not, explain why and what else you can do to achieve your goal _____

_____

_____

Other comments _____

_____

_____

_____

_____

_____

Daily Steps

Day 1 _____

Day 2 _____

Day 3 _____

Day 4 _____

Day 5 _____

Day 6 _____

Day 7 _____

Frank S. Adamo   frank@fsadamo.com   714-408-9287

Week 23

"Do not let what you cannot do interfere with what you can do."
— John Wooden

Do what you can do. Sometimes we must step back one step to go two steps forward. Other times, we need to take a break from one activity, until we are fresh with new ideas.

Your goal this week _____

_____

_____

_____

Did you accomplish your goal? Yes ☐ No ☐

If yes, how do you feel? _____

_____

_____

If not, explain why and what else you can do to achieve your goal _____

_____

_____

Other comments _____

_____

_____

_____

_____

_____

_____

Daily Steps
Day 1 _____
Day 2 _____
Day 3 _____
Day 4 _____
Day 5 _____
Day 6 _____
Day 7 _____

Frank S. Adamo   frank@fsadamo.com   714-408-9287

Week 24

"Go out on a limb - that's where the fruit is"

— Will Rogers

Step out of your comfort zone and take a chance.

Your goal this week _____

_____

_____

_____

Did you accomplish your goal? Yes ☐ No ☐

If yes, how do you feel? _____

_____

_____

If not, explain why and what else you can do to achieve your goal _____

_____

_____

Other comments _____

_____

_____

_____

_____

_____

_____

_____

Daily Steps

Day 1 _____

_____

_____

_____

Day 2 _____

_____

_____

_____

Day 3 _____

_____

_____

_____

Day 4 _____

_____

_____

_____

Day 5 _____

_____

_____

_____

Day 6 _____

_____

_____

_____

Day 7 _____

_____

_____

_____

Frank S. Adamo   frank@fsadamo.com   714-408-9287

Week 25

"Winning isn't everything, but wanting to win is."
— Vince Lombardi

In other words, it is the journey, not the destination that is important. We grow as we journey through our goals and aspirations. If we went straight to our destination, what would we have learned? Not much.

Your goal this week _____

_____

_____

_____

Did you accomplish your goal? Yes ☐ No ☐

If yes, how do you feel? _____

_____

_____

If not, explain why and what else you can do to achieve your goal _____

_____

_____

Other comments _____

_____

_____

_____

_____

_____

_____

Daily Steps
Day 1 _____
_____
_____
_____
Day 2 _____
_____
_____
_____
Day 3 _____
_____
_____
_____
Day 4 _____
_____
_____
_____
Day 5 _____
_____
_____
_____
Day 6 _____
_____
_____
_____
Day 7 _____
_____
_____
_____

Frank S. Adamo   frank@fsadamo.com   714-408-9287

Week 26

"Failures do what is tension relieving, while winners do what is goal achieving"

— Denis Waitley

First, I would never use the word "failure." Perhaps I would use "non-winners." From my perspective, we never fail even if we give up—as long as we learn from our experiences.

Your goal this week _____

_____

_____

_____

Did you accomplish your goal? Yes ☐ No ☐

If yes, how do you feel? _____

_____

_____

If not, explain why and what else you can do to achieve your goal _____

_____

_____

Other comments _____

_____

_____

_____

_____

_____

_____

Daily Steps

Day 1 _____

Day 2 _____

Day 3 _____

Day 4 _____

Day 5 _____

Day 6 _____

Day 7 _____

Frank S. Adamo frank@fsadamo.com 714-408-9287

Week 27

"What lies behind us, and what lies before us, are tiny matters compared to what lies within us."
— Ralph Waldo Emerson

Don't give up on your dreams. If you have achieved your dreams, dream again.

Your goal this week _____

_____

_____

_____

Did you accomplish your goal? Yes ☐ No ☐

If yes, how do you feel? _____

_____

_____

If not, explain why and what else you can do to achieve your goal _____

_____

_____

Other comments _____

_____

_____

_____

_____

_____

_____

Daily Steps

Day 1 _____
_____
_____
_____

Day 2 _____
_____
_____
_____

Day 3 _____
_____
_____
_____

Day 4 _____
_____
_____
_____

Day 5 _____
_____
_____
_____

Day 6 _____
_____
_____
_____

Day 7 _____
_____
_____
_____

Frank S. Adamo   frank@fsadamo.com   714-408-9287

Week 28

"Every ceiling, when reached, becomes a floor, upon which one walks as a matter of course and prescriptive right."
— Aldous Huxley

Don't stop setting goals and reaching them. Once you finished a goal, set another.

Your goal this week _____

_____

_____

_____

Did you accomplish your goal? Yes ☐ No ☐

If yes, how do you feel? _____

_____

_____

If not, explain why and what else you can do to achieve your goal _____

_____

_____

Other comments _____

_____

_____

_____

_____

_____

_____

Daily Steps
Day 1 _____
Day 2 _____
Day 3 _____
Day 4 _____
Day 5 _____
Day 6 _____
Day 7 _____

Frank S. Adamo   frank@fsadamo.com   714-408-9287

Week 29

"If you don't know where you are going, you'll end up someplace else."

— Yogi Berra

That's why we set goals, so that we know where we are going. There are many paths to travel from Los Angeles to New York, but we will get there if we know our destination. If not, we may travel aimlessly around the U.S. and never reach New York

Your goal this week _____

_____

_____

_____

Did you accomplish your goal? Yes ☐ No ☐

If yes, how do you feel? _____

_____

_____

If not, explain why and what else you can do to achieve your goal _____

_____

_____

Other comments _____

_____

_____

_____

_____

_____

Daily Steps

Day 1 _____

Day 2 _____

Day 3 _____

Day 4 _____

Day 5 _____

Day 6 _____

Day 7 _____

Frank S. Adamo frank@fsadamo.com 714-408-9287

Week 30

"Goals are dreams with deadlines."
— Diana Scharf Hunt

A goal must be a definable goal; otherwise, it's not a goal. It is merely a New Year's resolution. Saying "I want to lose weight this year" is not a goal; however, "I plan to lose 30 lbs. in 180 days from today" is a goal because it is specific.

Your goal this week _____

_____

_____

_____

Did you accomplish your goal? Yes ☐ No ☐

If yes, how do you feel? _____

_____

_____

If not, explain why and what else you can do to achieve your goal _____

_____

_____

Other comments _____

_____

_____

_____

_____

_____

_____

Daily Steps

Day 1 _____

_____

_____

_____

Day 2 _____

_____

_____

_____

Day 3 _____

_____

_____

_____

Day 4 _____

_____

_____

_____

Day 5 _____

_____

_____

_____

Day 6 _____

_____

_____

_____

Day 7 _____

_____

_____

_____

Frank S. Adamo   frank@fsadamo.com   714-408-9287

Week 31

"The important thing in life is to have a great aim, and the determination to attain it."

— Goethe

Setting a goal is like aiming a bow and arrow towards a distant target. It may take a few tries to hit a bull's eye, but as long as you have the determination to not give up, you eventually will do it.

Your goal this week _____

_____

_____

_____

Did you accomplish your goal? Yes ☐ No ☐

If yes, how do you feel? _____

_____

_____

If not, explain why and what else you can do to achieve your goal _____

_____

_____

Other comments _____

_____

_____

_____

_____

_____

_____

Frank S. Adamo   frank@fsadamo.com

Daily Steps

Day 1 _____

_____

_____

_____

Day 2 _____

_____

_____

_____

Day 3 _____

_____

_____

_____

Day 4 _____

_____

_____

_____

Day 5 _____

_____

_____

_____

Day 6 _____

_____

_____

_____

Day 7 _____

_____

_____

_____

714-408-9287

Week 32

"Destiny is no matter of chance. It is a matter of choice. It is not a thing to be waited for, it is a thing to be achieved."
— William Jennings Bryan

Be sure you stay focus on your vision and your plan (goals) to get there. Stay in the present while visualizing the finish line.

Your goal this week _____

_____

_____

_____

Did you accomplish your goal? Yes ☐ No ☐

If yes, how do you feel? _____

_____

_____

If not, explain why and what else you can do to achieve your goal _____

_____

_____

Other comments_____

_____

_____

_____

_____

_____

_____

Daily Steps
Day 1 _____
Day 2 _____
Day 3 _____
Day 4 _____
Day 5 _____
Day 6 _____
Day 7 _____

Frank S. Adamo   frank@fsadamo.com   714-408-9287

Week 33

"Long-range goals keep you from being frustrated by short-term failures."

— J.C. Penney

Be sure you stay focus on your vision and your plan (goals) to get there. Stay in the present while visualizing the finish line.

Your goal this week _____

_____

_____

_____

Did you accomplish your goal? Yes ☐ No ☐

If yes, how do you feel? _____

_____

_____

If not, explain why and what else you can do to achieve your goal _____

_____

_____

Other comments _____

_____

_____

_____

_____

_____

Daily Steps
Day 1 _____
Day 2 _____
Day 3 _____
Day 4 _____
Day 5 _____
Day 6 _____
Day 7 _____

Frank S. Adamo   frank@fsadamo.com   714-408-9287

Week 34

"Opportunity is missed by most people because it is dressed in overalls and looks like work."
— Thomas Edison,

The Law of Attraction signifies that we have to change our subconscious thoughts from negative to positive thoughts, then opportunities will come; yet, we can't just think it. We have to take action (i.e. work) to assure that these opportunities take place.

Your goal this week _____

_____

_____

_____

Did you accomplish your goal? Yes ☐ No ☐

If yes, how do you feel? _____

_____

_____

If not, explain why and what else you can do to achieve your goal _____

_____

_____

Other comments _____

_____

_____

_____

_____

_____

Daily Steps
Day 1 _____
Day 2 _____
Day 3 _____
Day 4 _____
Day 5 _____
Day 6 _____
Day 7 _____

Frank S. Adamo   frank@fsadamo.com   714-408-9287

Week 35

"Discipline is the bridge between goals and accomplishment."
— Jim Rohn

We can travel by car from Los Angeles to New York in about 5 days if we have disciplined ourselves and we made proper plans. If not, we may never make it to New York.

Your goal this week _____

_____

_____

_____

Did you accomplish your goal? Yes ☐ No ☐

If yes, how do you feel? _____

_____

_____

If not, explain why and what else you can do to achieve your goal _____

_____

_____

Other comments _____

_____

_____

_____

_____

_____

_____

Daily Steps
Day 1 _____
Day 2 _____
Day 3 _____
Day 4 _____
Day 5 _____
Day 6 _____
Day 7 _____

Frank S. Adamo   frank@fsadamo.com   714-408-9287

Week 36

"Learn from the past, set vivid, detailed goals for the future, and live in the only moment of time over which you have any control: now."
— Denis Waitley

Always learn from the past, otherwise we'll have the tendency to repeat it. Set goals from what you have learned from the past to assure that you don't repeat the same mistakes in the future.

Your goal this week _____

_____

_____

_____

Did you accomplish your goal? Yes ☐ No ☐

If yes, how do you feel? _____

_____

_____

If not, explain why and what else you can do to achieve your goal _____

_____

_____

Other comments _____

_____

_____

_____

_____

_____

_____

Daily Steps

Day 1 _____

_____

_____

_____

Day 2 _____

_____

_____

_____

Day 3 _____

_____

_____

_____

Day 4 _____

_____

_____

_____

Day 5 _____

_____

_____

_____

Day 6 _____

_____

_____

_____

Day 7 _____

_____

_____

_____

Frank S. Adamo   frank@fsadamo.com   714-408-9287

Week 37

"If you know what to do to reach your goal, it's not a big enough goal."

— Bob Proctor

Now you don't want to set an unreachable goal, such as reaching for the stars. Yet your goal needs purpose, imagination, and a sense of learning.

Your goal this week _____

_____

_____

_____

Did you accomplish your goal? Yes ☐ No ☐

If yes, how do you feel? _____

_____

_____

If not, explain why and what else you can do to achieve your goal _____

_____

_____

Other comments _____

_____

_____

_____

_____

_____

_____

Daily Steps
Day 1 _____
Day 2 _____
Day 3 _____
Day 4 _____
Day 5 _____
Day 6 _____
Day 7 _____

Frank S. Adamo   frank@fsadamo.com   714-408-9287

Week 38

"I don't know the key to success, but the key to failure is trying to please everybody."

— Bill Cosby

You need to please yourself first, and then concentrate only on those receptive to your ideas, dreams, and accomplishments. It's not worth the struggle to please everyone.

Your goal this week _____

_____

_____

_____

Did you accomplish your goal? Yes ☐ No ☐

If yes, how do you feel? _____

_____

_____

If not, explain why and what else you can do to achieve your goal _____

_____

_____

Other comments _____

_____

_____

_____

_____

_____

_____

Daily Steps

Day 1 _____

Day 2 _____

Day 3 _____

Day 4 _____

Day 5 _____

Day 6 _____

Day 7 _____

Frank S. Adamo   frank@fsadamo.com   714-408-9287

Week 39

"Your purpose explains what you are doing with your life. Your vision explains how you are living your purpose. Your goals enable you to realize your vision".

— Bob Proctor

Be sure you stay focus on your vision and your plan (goals) to get there. Stay in the present while visualizing the finish line.

Your goal this week _____

_____

_____

_____

Did you accomplish your goal? Yes ☐ No ☐

If yes, how do you feel? _____

_____

_____

If not, explain why and what else you can do to achieve your goal _____

_____

_____

Other comments _____

_____

_____

_____

_____

_____

_____

Daily Steps
Day 1 _____
_____
_____
Day 2 _____
_____
_____
Day 3 _____
_____
_____
Day 4 _____
_____
_____
Day 5 _____
_____
_____
Day 6 _____
_____
_____
Day 7 _____
_____
_____

Frank S. Adamo   frank@fsadamo.com   714-408-9287

Week 40

"All our dreams can come true – if we have the courage to pursue them"

— Walt Disney

We all have the potential for greatness. Though some have achieved greatness at a young age, others have had their dreams come true later in life. That is, it is never too late to fulfill your dreams.

Your goal this week _____

_____

_____

_____

Did you accomplish your goal? Yes ☐ No ☐

If yes, how do you feel? _____

_____

_____

If not, explain why and what else you can do to achieve your goal _____

_____

_____

Other comments _____

_____

_____

_____

_____

_____

_____

Daily Steps
Day 1 _____
Day 2 _____
Day 3 _____
Day 4 _____
Day 5 _____
Day 6 _____
Day 7 _____

Frank S. Adamo   frank@fsadamo.com   714-408-9287

Week 41

"No person will make a great business who wants to do it all himself or get all the credit."
— Andrew Carnegie

You need to work with others to achieve success. Good leadership is finding the right team to make you—and the team—successful. And a good leader will never accept all the credit for a project and will never blame others for mistakes that occurred on his/her watch.

Your goal this week _____

_____

_____

_____

Did you accomplish your goal? Yes ☐ No ☐

If yes, how do you feel? _____

_____

_____

If not, explain why and what else you can do to achieve your goal _____

_____

_____

Other comments _____

_____

_____

_____

_____

_____

Daily Steps
Day 1 _____
Day 2 _____
Day 3 _____
Day 4 _____
Day 5 _____
Day 6 _____
Day 7 _____

Frank S. Adamo   frank@fsadamo.com   714-408-9287

Week 42

"All of us tend to put off living. We are all dreaming of some magical rose garden over the horizon – instead of enjoying the roses that are blooming outside our windows today."
— Dale Carnegie

Sometimes you must travel to find your dreams, yet opportunities flourish everywhere. For example, you purchase a brand new car and you choose a particular model—and color—because you don't want to be like everyone else. Then, once purchased, you see the same exact mode, and color, everywhere you go. Opportunities to reach your dreams are there, you simply need to become aware of them.

Your goal this week _____

_____

_____

_____

Did you accomplish your goal? Yes ☐ No ☐

If yes, how do you feel? _____

_____

_____

If not, explain why and what else you can do to achieve your goal _____

_____

_____

Other comments _____

_____

_____

_____

_____

Daily Steps

Day 1 _____

Day 2 _____

Day 3 _____

Day 4 _____

Day 5 _____

Day 6 _____

Day 7 _____

Frank S. Adamo frank@fsadamo.com 714-408-9287

Week 43

"The start is what stops most people."

— Don Shula

In physics we have inertia, the resistance of a body to changes in its momentum, i.e. a body at rest remains at rest, and a body in motion continues moving in a straight line and at a constant speed, unless a force is applied to it. Likewise, to start a project, task, or goal, we need some sort of force to start; such as a dream, a goal and commitment. In turn, we need to stay dedicated and focused; otherwise, outside forces may derail our intent.

Your goal this week _____

_____

_____

_____

Did you accomplish your goal? Yes ☐ No ☐

If yes, how do you feel? _____

_____

_____

If not, explain why and what else you can do to achieve your goal _____

_____

_____

Other comments _____

_____

_____

_____

_____

Daily Steps
Day 1 _____
Day 2 _____
Day 3 _____
Day 4 _____
Day 5 _____
Day 6 _____
Day 7 _____

Frank S. Adamo   frank@fsadamo.com   714-408-9287

Week 44

"No amount of reading or memorizing will make you successful in life. It is the understanding and application of wise thought which counts."

— Bob Proctor

Have you ever seen anyone learn to ride a bike or drive a car merely by reading and memorizing? You need to practice. Better yet, would you want to have a surgeon operate on you without having gone through internship and residency?

Your goal this week _____

_____

_____

_____

Did you accomplish your goal? Yes ☐ No ☐

If yes, how do you feel? _____

_____

_____

If not, explain why and what else you can do to achieve your goal _____

_____

_____

Other comments _____

_____

_____

_____

_____

Daily Steps
Day 1 _____
Day 2 _____
Day 3 _____
Day 4 _____
Day 5 _____
Day 6 _____
Day 7 _____

Frank S. Adamo   frank@fsadamo.com   714-408-9287

Week 45

"Wrong turns are as important as right turns. More important, sometimes."

— Anonymous

We learn and grow through the wrong turns in life. Thus, don't be concerned about making wrong turns, as long as you learn from them and get back on track.

Your goal this week _____

_____

_____

_____

Did you accomplish your goal? Yes ☐ No ☐

If yes, how do you feel? _____

_____

_____

If not, explain why and what else you can do to achieve your goal _____

_____

_____

Other comments _____

_____

_____

_____

_____

_____

_____

Daily Steps
Day 1 _____
Day 2 _____
Day 3 _____
Day 4 _____
Day 5 _____
Day 6 _____
Day 7 _____

Frank S. Adamo   frank@fsadamo.com   714-408-9287

Week 46

"How to discover your greatness? By upgrading our relationships and by having goals beyond our comfort zone."
— Les Brown

We shouldn't set goals which are unreachable, yet we shouldn't set goals which keep us within our comfort zone; otherwise, we will never reach our destination and achieve our dreams.

Your goal this week _____

_____

_____

_____

Did you accomplish your goal? Yes ☐ No ☐

If yes, how do you feel? _____

_____

_____

If not, explain why and what else you can do to achieve your goal _____

_____

_____

Other comments _____

_____

_____

_____

_____

_____

_____

Frank S. Adamo   frank@fsadamo.com

Daily Steps

Day 1 _____

_____

_____

_____

Day 2 _____

_____

_____

_____

Day 3 _____

_____

_____

_____

Day 4 _____

_____

_____

_____

Day 5 _____

_____

_____

_____

Day 6 _____

_____

_____

_____

Day 7 _____

_____

_____

_____

714-408-9287

Week 47

"When obstacles arise change your direction to reach your goal, not the decision to get there.

— Zig Ziglar

Be your own GPS. If you have to make a detour or you missed your right turn, your GPS will re-adjust and put you back on track to your destination. Likewise, step over, go around, shovel through, do whatever it takes to get through your obstacles. Then, get back on track. Your GPS never quits. Don't you.

Your goal this week _____

_____

_____

_____

Did you accomplish your goal? Yes ☐ No ☐

If yes, how do you feel? _____

_____

_____

If not, explain why and what else you can do to achieve your goal _____

_____

_____

Other comments _____

_____

_____

_____

_____

Daily Steps
Day 1 _____
Day 2 _____
Day 3 _____
Day 4 _____
Day 5 _____
Day 6 _____
Day 7 _____

Frank S. Adamo   frank@fsadamo.com   714-408-9287

Week 48

"I believe this with all my heart. If you don't enjoy your way through the challenge, the end result will not be worth all the hassle."
— Loraine Borg

With all the challenges we have had and will continue to have, accept them and look at them as learning experiences and growth opportunities.

Your goal this week _____

_____

_____

_____

Did you accomplish your goal? Yes ☐   No ☐

If yes, how do you feel? _____

_____

_____

If not, explain why and what else you can do to achieve your goal _____

_____

_____

Other comments _____

_____

_____

_____

_____

_____

_____

Frank S. Adamo   frank@fsadamo.com   714-408-9287

Daily Steps

Day 1 _____

Day 2 _____

Day 3 _____

Day 4 _____

Day 5 _____

Day 6 _____

Day 7 _____

Week 49

"It is not enough to take steps which may some day lead to a goal; each step must be itself a goal and a step likewise."
— Johann Wolfgang von Goethe

The purpose of the column on the right is to evaluate the daily steps to achieving your weekly goal.

Your goal this week _____

_____

_____

_____

Did you accomplish your goal? Yes ☐ No ☐

If yes, how do you feel? _____

_____

_____

If not, explain why and what else you can do to achieve your goal _____

_____

_____

Other comments _____

_____

_____

_____

_____

_____

Daily Steps
Day 1 _____
Day 2 _____
Day 3 _____
Day 4 _____
Day 5 _____
Day 6 _____
Day 7 _____

Frank S. Adamo   frank@fsadamo.com   714-408-9287

Week 50

"It is literally true that you can succeed best and quickest by helping others to succeed."

— Napoleon Hill

As you set your goals, determine how others may benefit. Help them achieve their own goals by showing them how you are following your goals. If you can help them, they will help you.

Your goal this week _____

_____

_____

_____

Did you accomplish your goal? Yes ☐ No ☐

If yes, how do you feel? _____

_____

_____

If not, explain why and what else you can do to achieve your goal _____

_____

_____

Other comments _____

_____

_____

_____

_____

_____

_____

Daily Steps
Day 1 _____
Day 2 _____
Day 3 _____
Day 4 _____
Day 5 _____
Day 6 _____
Day 7 _____

Frank S. Adamo   frank@fsadamo.com   714-408-9287

Week 51

"You were born to win, but to be a winner, you must plan to win, prepare to win, and expect to win."

— Zig Ziglar

Not only were you born to win. From the moment of conception, when that one sperm, out of millions of others, impregnated the egg that began your life, you were the winner of the biggest race of your life. Thus, always plan to win, prepare to win, and expect to win. It will never be as difficult as your original race when you had to compete with millions of others. You are, indeed, a winner.

Your goal this week _____

_____

_____

Did you accomplish your goal? Yes ☐ No ☐

If yes, how do you feel? _____

_____

If not, explain why and what else you can do to achieve your goal _____

_____

_____

Other comments _____

_____

_____

_____

_____

Daily Steps
Day 1 _____
Day 2 _____
Day 3 _____
Day 4 _____
Day 5 _____
Day 6 _____
Day 7 _____

Frank S. Adamo   frank@fsadamo.com   714-408-9287

Week 52

"Pressure is a word that is misused in our vocabulary. When you start thinking of pressure, it's because you've started to think of failure."

— Tommy Lasorda

When you start to feel pressured, restructure your thinking. Throw out the negative thoughts of pressure and failure. If you have hit a detour, remember your GPS, recalculate a way around your detour.

Your goal this week _____

_____

_____

_____

Did you accomplish your goal? Yes ☐ No ☐

If yes, how do you feel? _____

_____

_____

If not, explain why and what else you can do to achieve your goal _____

_____

_____

_____

Other comments _____

_____

_____

_____

_____

_____

Daily Steps
Day 1 _____
_____
_____
_____
Day 2 _____
_____
_____
_____
Day 3 _____
_____
_____
_____
Day 4 _____
_____
_____
_____
Day 5 _____
_____
_____
_____
Day 6 _____
_____
_____
_____
Day 7 _____
_____
_____
_____

Frank S. Adamo   frank@fsadamo.com   714-408-9287

Author Index

Author	Week
Abraham Lincoln	4
Al Batt	22
Aldous Huxley	28
Andrew Carnegie	41
Anonymous	19, 45
Bill Cosby	38
Bob Proctor	37, 39, 44
C Popplestown	5
Carlos Castaneda	11
Dale Carnegie	42
Denis Waitley	18, 26, 36
Diana Scharf Hunt	30
Don Shula	43
Doris Mortman	12
Eleanor Roosevelt	7
Goethe	31
Henry Ford	6
J.C. Penney	33
Jim Rohn	10, 35
Johann Wolfgang von Goethe	49
John Wooden	23
Katherine Dunham	2
Kathleen Norris	8
Kenichi Ohmae	13
Larry Elder	15
Leonardo da Vinci	16
Les Brown	46
Loraine Borg	48
Louise Hay	21
Margaret Thatcher	14
Max Lucado	1
Napoleon Hill	50
Ralph Waldo Emerson	27
Ralph Wardo Emerson	17
Reinhold Niebuhr	3
Scott Reed	9
Thomas Edison	8, 34
Tom Peters	20
Tommy Lasorda	52
Vince Lombardi	25
Walt Disney	40
Will Rogers	24
William Jennings Bryan	32
Yogi Berra	29
Zig Ziglar	47, 51

Frank S. Adamo   frank@fsadamo.com   714-408-9287